There's something magical...

...about the home of Liverpool FC, the most successful football club in the history of English football.

A total of 18 league titles, 5 European Cups, 7 FA Cups, 7 League Cups, 3 UEFA Cups and 3 European Super Cups have been brought back to Anfield, one of world football's most iconic, atmospheric stadiums.

No other English club can match that haul of silverware. No other club has won as many matches in the top flight of English football. No other club has been champions of Europe three times in five years. No other club is Liverpool.

Anfield's story started back in 1884 when it was the home of Everton Football Club, founder members of the Football League.

Everton played Earlestown in the first ever game held on the ground, but it wasn't long before Anfield was home to a new club.

A dispute between local brewer John Houlding, who as well as owning Anfield was the president of Everton, and other club members over a rent increase and a plan to only sell his brand of beer on a match day saw a split.

It resulted in Everton moving to a new home at Goodison Park and Houlding setting up a new club – Liverpool FC. It was the best decision he ever made!

On September 1 1892, Liverpool played their first game at Anfield, beating Rotherham 7-1. LFC were members of the Football League within a season, had adopted the now famous red shirts before the turn of the century and were champions of England for the first time in 1901.

The first league title win was the start of a success story that is unparalleled in English football, although it took the appointment of Bill Shankly as manager in December 1959 to be the catalyst for that success.

Above the tunnel inside Anfield is the famous sign that Shankly put up.

"It's there to remind our lads who they're playing for," he said, "and to remind the opposition who they're playing against."

Anfield has witnessed countless great games. It has been home to some of the greatest teams ever to grace a football field, the greatest managers in the game and, on the Kop, some of the most passionate, noisy, partisan supporters in the world.

It has seen joy and despair. Heroes and villains. Goals and glory. Titles and tears. Moments that pass in the twinkling of an eye, but last in the memory for a lifetime. Moments that Kopites live for.

Anfield is a cathedral to Liverpool supporters – a place of worship and joy, but also a shrine to those who lost their lives at Hillsborough in 1989.

Most of all, the stadium that stands between Anfield Road and Walton Breck Road in Liverpool 4 is home. Our home.

This is Anfield...

CONTENTS

LFC Museum & Stadium Tour

Date of Tour:01/06/2010

Time of Tour 13:00

Price level:Standard

Please keep this ticket with
you at all times

HONOURS

LEAGUE CHAMPIONS
1900/01 1905/06 1921/22
1922/23 1946/47 1963/64
1965/66 1972/73 1975/76 1976/77
1978/79 1979/80 1981/82 1982/83
1983/84 1985/86 1987/88
1989/90

EUROPEAN CUP WINNERS
1976/77 1977/78 1980/81 1983/84
2004/05

EUROPEAN SUPER CUP WINNERS
1977/78 2001/02 2005/06

UEFA CUP WINNERS
1972/73 1975/76 2000/01

FA CUP WINNERS
1964/65 1973/74 1985/86 1988/89
1991/92 2000/01 2005/06

LEAGUE CUP WINNERS
1980/81 1981/82 1982/83 1983/84
1994/95 2000/01 2002/03

COMMUNITY SHIELD WINNERS
1966 1974 1976 1979 1980 1982
1988 1989 2001 2006

Published by

Sport Media

Part of a Trinity Mirror Business

LEGENDS

THE MEN WHO SHAPED THE HISTORY OF ANFIELD

THE LEGENDARY LIVERPOOL PLAYERS

SINCE 1892, almost 700 players have appeared for Liverpool Football Club.

Amongst them are some of the greatest players to have ever graced football pitches both in England and abroad.

We've had so many legends at Anfield that entire books have been written about them, so trying to mention all the Liverpool stars of past and present would be impossible.

However, there are many that we simply cannot fail to mention, and where better to start than with the three players generally regarded as the greatest of them all.

Flying Scottish winger *Billy Liddell* scored 228 goals for Liverpool and was so exciting to watch that fans came to see him as much as they did the team during the bleak 1950s period. »

Billy Liddell

Glorious Managers

THE LEADERS WHO GUIDED LIVERPOOL TO TRIUMPH »

IF there is one man who stands above all others as being the most famous figure in Liverpool Football Club's history then it is *Bill Shankly*.

The club had enjoyed success under previous managers, ever since our first bosses *John McKenna* and *W E Barclay* won a couple of Second Division titles between them in 1894 and 1896.

Tom Watson guided us to our first league titles in 1901 and 1906, *David Ashworth* brought the championship back to Anfield in 1922, *Matt McQueen* repeated the trick in 1923 and *George Kay* was in charge when Liverpool became the first post-war champions of England in 1947.

But it was the appointment of charismatic Scot Shankly in December 1959 that transformed Liverpool FC from Second Division also-rans into the most successful club in the history of English football.

Shankly didn't just overhaul the team by bringing in revolution cornerstones Ian St John and Ron Yeats, he instilled a new attitude and spirit inside the club.

He persuaded the board to improve the facilities at both Melwood and Anfield. He had the famous This Is Anfield sign installed above the tunnel to inspire his players, and introduced our now famous all-red strip because he felt it struck a psychological blow by making his players look bigger.

Shanks also made his players believe they were playing for the greatest club in the world and, just as significantly, harnessed the power of the Kop through his unique bond with the Liverpool supporters.

Shankly, who hailed from a working-class mining family in Glenbuck, Scotland, made Kopites believe that they were just as important as the

players. He tapped into the Liverpudlian psyche, channelling Scouse passion, pride and cockiness into his 12th man. He made the Anfield crowd realise that through their vocal backing and partisan support, they could inspire their team and frighten opponents to death.

And so, with an inspirational manager at the helm, great players on the pitch and intense backing on the terraces, Liverpool rose from the Second Division in 1962 to become league champions in 1964 and 1966.

Between those successes, Shankly guided the Reds to their first ever FA Cup triumph at Wembley in 1965, and led Liverpool into European competition for the first time.

That Wembley triumph meant as much as the league titles to Kopites, as it put an end to Evertonian taunts that Liverpool had never won the cup.

Shankly built a second great team in the 1970s. The likes of Kevin Keegan and Ray Clemence were brought in from lower-league clubs and turned into stars as Shanks landed his third league title in 1973.

He also guided Liverpool to their first piece of European silverware that season – the UEFA Cup – and in 1974 the Reds returned to Wembley to lift another FA Cup.

But, to the shock of the footballing world and the devastation of Kopites, Shankly decided to quit Anfield that summer, citing tiredness.

People feared it would be the beginning of the end for the Liverpool success story, but they hadn't reckoned on his trusted lieutenant *Bob Paisley*, a member of Shankly's famous bootroom, taking Liverpool to even greater »

GREAT ANFIELD GOALSCORERS

It was another Scot, *Kenny Dalglish*, who eventually challenged Liddell for the crown as Liverpool's greatest ever player. King Kenny netted 172 goals for the Reds and producing some of the finest performances ever seen at Anfield.

Steven Gerrard, the only man to have ever scored in the European Cup, UEFA Cup, FA Cup and League Cup finals, is now fighting Kenny for that honour thanks to his numerous inspirational performances, not least in Istanbul in 2005 and Cardiff in 2006.

Speaking of cup finals, no one can match the goalscoring exploits of *Ian Rush*, Liverpool's all-time

leading goalscorer on 346 goals and a man who has netted a record five goals in FA Cup finals alone.

Rushie is far from the only goalscoring hero the Kop have had down the years.

Roger Hunt, christened 'Sir Roger' by Kopites in the 1960s, scored a club record 245 league goals for Liverpool, while South African striker *Gordon Hodgson* struck 233 top-flight league goals in the 1920s and 1930s, another Reds record.

Robbie Fowler was perhaps the most natural born goalscorer we've ever had, and was nicknamed 'God' because he could do no wrong in front of goal, netting 183 times for the Reds.

Harry Chambers, *Sam Raybould*, *Jack Parkinson* and *Dick Forshaw* were all noted goalscorers of yesteryear, while *Jack Balmer*, who scored 111 times for Liverpool, remains unique in Football League history for »

Trophy haul: Bob Paisley and his team

success. Paisley, a softly spoken man from Hetton-le-Hole, made 278 appearances for the club as a player but didn't want the manager's job and tried to talk Shanks into staying.

That was just about the only thing Paisley didn't achieve as he led Liverpool Football Club to an astonishing 19 pieces of silverware in just nine seasons.

He didn't win anything in his first season but followed that up by clinching both the league title and UEFA Cup in 1976.

A year later, Paisley guided Liverpool to a first ever European Cup success. His side beat Borussia Moenchengladbach in Rome on a night that many older Kopites still regard as the greatest in Liverpool FC's illustrious history.

The Reds were also league champions in 1977, and only missed out on an unprecedented treble by losing the FA Cup final to Manchester United – the FA Cup would be the only trophy Bob failed to win as Liverpool manager.

In the following seasons, Paisley signed all-time greats such as Kenny Dalglish, Alan Hansen, Graeme Souness and Ian Rush, and the trophies kept on coming to Anfield.

Between 1978 and 1983, Bob's team won four more league titles (1979, 1980, 1982, 1983), two more European Cups – at Wembley (1978) and in Paris (1981), three League Cups (1981, 1982, 1983) and the European Super Cup (1978).

Throw in the five Charity Shields Liverpool also won, and by the time Paisley retired in 1983, he was the most successful manager in the history of English football and to this day remains the only boss to have led a team to three European Cup successes – a remarkable achievement given he did so in just a five-season spell. »

scoring hat-tricks in three consecutive games in 1946.

Liverpool's superb current number nine *Fernando Torres* became the first player since Balmer to score consecutive hat-tricks for Liverpool in the league, and as the striker who netted 50 league goals for the club in the fewest number of games, he's had Kopites bouncing time and time again.

09

Ian St John also scored more than 100 goals for the club, one of which was the Reds' first FA Cup final winner in 1965, while other Johns who knew where the goal was include *John Toshack* and *John Aldridge*.

John Barnes not only netted 108 times for Liverpool, but in the late 1980s turned in some of the most magnificent, exciting and skilful performances ever seen in a red shirt. »

WINGERS AND RECORD BREAKERS

Stevie Heighway used to be on the same wing before Barnes and was a Kop favourite for his dribbling skills, while in the 1990s *Steve McManaman* left defenders trying to pick the knots out of their legs at full-time. *Peter Thompson* was adept at destroying full-backs in a similar style in the '60s.

Ian Callaghan is a name that will forever be associated with Liverpool FC, as no one is likely to ever beat his astonishing 857-appearance record, while right-back *Phil Neal*'s status as the club's most decorated player, with eight league titles and four European Cups (amongst others) in his medal collection, is going to take some surpassing. Neal also played 417 games in a row – a club record.

Alan Hansen also had an unbelievable Anfield career, winning almost as many medals as Neal and captaining Liverpool to the league and FA Cup double in 1986. »

Tricky job: Joe Fagan succeeded Bob Paisley, and promptly won a treble in his first year

As they had done when Shanks stepped down, Liverpool's board appointed from within when Paisley retired, and assistant manager *Joe Fagan* took charge.

Incredibly, the Scouser managed to achieve something Paisley didn't in just his first campaign – he became the first British manager to win three major trophies in a season.

Fagan led Liverpool to the league title, League Cup and a fourth European Cup in 1984, one of the most under-rated achievements in English football.

He was unable to repeat that success the following year, and even before the tragedy of Heysel, the 64-year-old had decided to retire.

His replacement was Liverpool's greatest player of them all, *Kenny Dalglish*.

King Kenny became the club's first player/manager and created history in his first season in charge when he guided Liverpool to a league and FA Cup double.

It was the first time the club had won the two trophies in the same campaign, and the season had a fairytale finish with Kenny himself scoring the goal at Chelsea that won the league, and the Reds beating Everton at Wembley in the first all-Merseyside FA Cup final.

Kenny's title-winning side of 1988 played arguably the most attractive football in the club's history, and Liverpool's 18th championship was landed in 1990.

Between those triumphs came the trauma of 1989 and the Hillsborough disaster. »

TEAM CAPTAINS AND LEADERS

WE'VE had many inspirational captains down the years, including three men who lifted the European Cup on four occasions between 1977 and 1984.

The all-action *Emlyn Hughes* skippered the Reds in Rome '77 and Wembley '78; local lad *Phil Thompson* lived the dream in 1981 when he wore the armband in Paris.

Graeme Souness is arguably the finest central midfielder in Liverpool's history, and it was he who led us into the lion's den in Rome '84 and lifted the European Cup aloft after AS Roma were beaten on their own turf.

Eleven years earlier, 'Anfield Iron' *Tommy Smith* had become the first Liverpool captain to lift a European trophy when he got his hands on the UEFA Cup, while big *Ron Yeats* was our first FA Cup-winning skipper in the 1960s.

Another commanding centre-half, *Alex Raisbeck*, skippered Liverpool to our first two league titles, and full-back *Donald MacKinlay* was the man with the armband in the back-to-back championship wins in the 1920s.

The versatile *Steve Nicol* was so important to Liverpool in the 1980s that he was voted Footballer of the Year, a rare accomplishment for a full-back. Another key member of the team during that decade was *Ronnie Whelan*, who had a happy knack of scoring vital goals from midfield in big games.

Giant Finn *Sami Hyypia* earned himself a reputation as one of our finest centre-halves during a decade of service at Anfield in the Noughties. »

11

"Kenny ohhh Kenny... I'd walk a million miles for one of your goals"

From 'Every Other Sunday'
Traditional Kop song

OTHER GREAT ANFIELD STARS

Liverpool is also renowned for having had some of the finest goalkeepers in the game.

Ulsterman *Elisha Scott*'s duels with Everton's legendary Dixie Dean in the 1920s are the stuff of Merseyside derby folklore, while the 'flying pig' *Tommy Lawrence* was Bill Shankly's number one before *Ray Clemence*.

Clem made 665 appearances for Liverpool, a club record for a goalkeeper, and is widely regarded as our best ever 'keeper.

Bruce Grobbelaar's wobbly legs in Rome and *Jerzy Dudek*'s copycat performance in Istanbul earned them cult status on the Kop, and present custodian *Pepe Reina* has already set so many records for clean sheets that he is being talked of in the same breath as Clemence.

Jamie Carragher is another current hero who will go down as an all-time great and one of Liverpool's finest ever defenders, while *Chris Lawler* scored an amazing 61 goals from right-back, all of them from open play!

Gerry Byrne was a hard-as-nails full-back in the 1960s, best summed up by the way he played almost the entire '65 FA Cup final with a broken collarbone!

Left-back *Alan Kennedy* fired home Liverpool's winning goal in the 1981 European Cup final against Real Madrid and the winning penalty in Rome three years later.

Namesake *Ray Kennedy* was converted from a striker to an attacking midfielder by Bob Paisley with such success that Liverpool fielded more enquiries for him than any other player in the 1970s – an indication of how good he was when you consider he played in the same team as *Kevin Keegan*.

Keegan was perhaps Liverpool's first megastar, with his commitment, power and goals making him a huge fans' favourite.

More recently, *Dietmar Hamann* became a Kop cult hero as a result of some fine midfield performances and his Scouse-German accent – a variation on big *Jan Molby*'s Danish Scouse. Many Reds believe that 'Didi' finally replaced midfield powerhouse *Steve McMahon*, a vital cog in the Liverpool engine room in the late '80s.

Liverpool would never »

Above: Look of concern: Kenny Dalglish at the fateful Hillsborough Cup tie

Above right: Graeme Souness and Roy Evans issuing orders

Far right: Rafa Benitez lifts the Champions League trophy with pride in 2005

Dalglish led the club magnificently through that period, attending as many of the funerals as he possibly could and standing up to defend Liverpool supporters who had been subjected to scandalous, scurrilous accusations by a tabloid newspaper.

He also led his players to the FA Cup final, which was won after another victory over Everton, and only a last-minute Arsenal goal in the final league match of the season at Anfield prevented Kenny from completing a double-double.

The stress of leading Liverpool through that period finally caught up with Kenny in 1991, and he resigned after a frantic 4-4 FA Cup draw against Everton.

Former skipper **Graeme Souness** replaced Kenny, but although he landed the FA Cup in 1992, there were many poor results during his time in charge at Anfield. He was replaced in 1994 by a member of Shankly's old bootroom, **Roy Evans**.

Liverpool played some good football under Evans but the only silverware they had to show for it was the 1995 League Cup, so former French international **Gerard Houllier** was brought in to work alongside Roy in the summer of 1998.

The partnership didn't work out and Houllier took sole command later that year, sparking a new revolution.

Houllier brought an international flavour to Anfield, attracting players from across Europe such as Sami Hyypia and Didi Hamann, and in 2001 his side won a unique treble of FA Cup, League Cup and UEFA Cup, before qualifying for the Champions League for the first time.

have won a fifth European Cup without the key contributions of Spanish duo *Xabi Alonso* and *Luis Garcia*, and other midfielders who are remembered for important performances and vital goals include *Terry McDermott, Brian Hall, Jimmy Case, Sammy Lee, Danny Murphy, Gordon Milne, Ray Houghton, Geoff Strong, Vladimir Smicer* and *Gary McAllister*.

Men like *Ronnie Moran, Laurie Hughes, Mark Lawrenson, Stephane Henchoz, Gary Gillespie, Steve Finnan* and *Alec Lindsay* defended like their lives depended on it.

Having not won a European trophy since 1984, that season put Liverpool back on the European map, but only the European Super Cup and another League Cup (2003) were added to the trophy cabinet by Houllier so it was time for another change.

In the summer of 2004, Houllier was replaced by **Rafael Benitez**, a Spaniard who had taken Valencia to two surprise La Liga titles in three seasons, and a UEFA Cup success.

What followed defied belief as despite the inevitable season of transition that followed, Rafa led a Steven Gerrard and Jamie Carragher-inspired Liverpool to a remarkable fifth European Cup success. After being 3-0 down at half-time to AC Milan in Istanbul, the Reds came back to draw 3-3 and win on penalties in the most amazing Champions League final of them all.

A year later, another trophy followed, this time the FA Cup, and the European Super Cup was also added to the cabinet.

With top players like Pepe Reina and Fernando Torres brought to the club by Rafa, Liverpool narrowly missed out on their first Premier League title in 2009, becoming the first side to only lose two games all season but fail to win the league.

As ever, the pursuit of trophies, something every Liverpool manager is judged by, goes on.

In total, 17 men have managed Liverpool Football Club, and 14 of them have brought silverware to Anfield. It's a success rate of which we are very, very proud.

Unique treble: Houllier with the UEFA Cup in 2001

And at the other end of the pitch, goals from the likes of *David Fairclough, David Johnson, Peter Beardsley* and *Albert Stubbins* – who famously appeared on the cover of The Beatles' Sergeant Pepper's Lonely Hearts Club Band album – contributed to the Liverpool FC success story.

So too did many, many others, including a couple of players who were great friends and went on to make a name for themselves as managers – *Sir Matt Busby* and Bob Paisley.

As far as legends go, few clubs if any have more of them than Liverpool.

13

Television studio

When an Anfield game is televised live, this is the studio where presenters and pundits gather to analyse the Reds.

Anfield Road
Capacity: 9,116

Visitors' allocation

Visiting fans are allocated the bottom corner of the lower tier in the Anfield Road end on a matchday, but their allocation isn't always the same. Away clubs can opt to take a minimum of 791 tickets and a maximum of 2,948 tickets, depending on how many they think they will sell.

Pitch width: 68m
Pitch length: 101m

The Pitch
95% Grass
5% Artificial

Main Stand
Capacity: 9,575

Paddock
Capacity: 2,454

Executive Boxes

Capacity: 344

Centenary Stand

Capacity: 11,411

The Kop

Capacity: 12,390

Scoreboard

Anfield famously never had a scoreboard until this electronic one was installed in the corner of the Centenary Stand in November 2003. The highest number it has reached (so far!) is eight, on the night when Liverpool beat Besiktas 8-0 in a UEFA Champions League game in 2007.

PROFESSIONAL GRASS

A VIEW TO A THRILL FROM THE DIRECTORS' BOX

RED AND WHITE...
AND LOTS OF LIGHTS

IT is every Liverpool fan's dream to wear the red shirt and step onto the hallowed Anfield turf.

Renowned for being the best pitch in England, any player who steps on it is treading in the footsteps of legends.

The pitch measures 101m x 68m, as do most others in the Premier League, but there is none better to play on.

It is made of 95% natural grass and 5% artificial turf, which helps to knit the surface together.

A team of groundsmen, assistants and apprentices ensure bad weather or fungal diseases do not ruin the pitch. Their job is to prepare and repair.

As well as the traditional tools of the trade (pitchforks, rakes, mowers, etc), the club also utilises a mobile lighting system.

The 10 units are placed on the pitch 24 hours a day during winter and are only taken off for matches and mowing.

Anfield stadium manager Ged Poynton explains: "Our aim is to produce a playing surface of good quality in the winter months when normally it is at its worst.

"It's a total control system whereby measurements taken by mini weather stations on the surface help the groundsman decide when to apply water and fertiliser to optimise grass growth."

Anfield's mobile lighting system in action

"It's great grass at Anfield, professional grass"

Bill Shankly

ISN'T THAT...?
FAMOUS FACES TO GRACE THE BOX

THE best view of Anfield and the comfiest seats can be found in the directors' box.

This is where the great and the good sit, looking out onto the magnificent pitch in front of them.

It is the most prestigious section in the ground and has played host to a number of famous people over the years.

James Bond is among them. Actor **Daniel Craig**, who has played Bond in Casino Royale and Quantum of Solace, was brought up in Chester and is a lifelong Liverpool supporter.

Other well-known names to have dropped in include the **Crown Prince of Brunei,** singer **Rod Stewart**, racing driver **Nigel Mansell**, singer **Chris de Burgh** and politician **Michael Howard**.

Royalty has graced Anfield too, although not actually in the directors' box. **The Queen** and the **Duke of Edinburgh** made an official visit in 1993 while, more recently, **Prince Charles** and the **Duchess of Cornwall** came for a Prince's Trust event.

Henry Kissinger, the former US secretary of state and thus one of the most powerful people on earth, arrived at short notice while in the city to give a university lecture.

He was shown around Anfield by former Liverpool player Brian Hall who recalls that Kissinger was "absolutely transfixed". He adds: "I couldn't get him off the pitch."

Many opposition managers like to watch the game from the elevated view the directors' box provides, but that's rarely been the case for Liverpool's bosses. Bill Shankly was an exception.

It is situated in the Main Stand, which is the oldest part of the ground and was last redeveloped in 1973.

Directly opposite is the Centenary Stand, which was created when a second tier was added to the old Kemlyn Road stand. It was completed in 1992, 100 years since the birth of the club.

To the left is the Anfield Road end, which was extended to two tiers in 1997. Visiting supporters are situated here and, for league games, their clubs are allocated between 791 and 2,948 tickets.

Of course, the most famous stand of all is the Kop. Created in 1906, it was the most famous football terrace in the world and has retained its reputation for noise and passion since being rebuilt as an all-seater stand in 1994.

Anfield's record attendance is 61,095, set on February 2 1952 for an FA Cup fourth-round tie against Wolves. We won 2-1 and Bob Paisley scored!

FROM BOOTROOM TO PRESS ROOM
ANFIELD'S MYSTICAL INNER SANCTUM

Bootroom boy to man:
Bob Paisley was one of Bill
Shankly's bootroom boys
(below), and he continued
where his predecessor left off –
here he is in the bootroom with
the league trophy in 1977

Anfield HQ: Both Bob Paisley and Roy Evans used the bootroom as an unofficial office while on the coaching staff at Liverpool. It was here that they would discuss tactics with their colleagues and plot the downfall of their opponents

The Bootroom Boys

THE WINDOWLESS ROOM WHERE AN EMPIRE WAS BUILT »

ONE of the most mystical places relating to Liverpool is the cramped bootroom that once stood within the Main Stand at Anfield.

A windowless bunker off the dressing room corridor, it was where the management and coaching staff would retire to discuss players, opponents and matches in private.

It was created, almost accidentally, by Liverpool coach and future manager Joe Fagan in the 1960s when Bill Shankly was manager.

Together with fellow backroom team members Bob Paisley and Reuben Bennett, he wanted somewhere in the ground where they could talk football and invite opposition coaches for an after-match drink.

Fagan had been given some crates of Guinness Export as a gift by local councillor Paul Orr. At the time Orr managed an amateur side called Guiness (sic) Export, and Fagan had allowed their players to use the Anfield treatment room.

The crates had been placed in the room where players' boots hung off pegs and Fagan turned them on their side, so they could be used as makeshift seats.

The bootroom's simplicity and the common sense spoke within came to symbolise the values of the club. For 30 years it served as the area where Liverpool's coaches would gather, and it entered folklore as the secret behind the success.

As well as Shankly (an occasional visitor), Paisley, Fagan and Bennett, other

men who in time would use it as an unofficial office included Ronnie Moran, Roy Evans, youth development officer Tom Saunders, coach John Bennison and chief scout Geoff Twentyman. Collectively they became known as the bootroom boys.

Later on, former Reds Chris Lawler, Ron Yeats, Phil Thompson and (manager) Kenny Dalglish joined the coaching staff and were afforded a privilege that didn't come their way as players – entry to the inner sanctum.

Ronnie Moran recalled how they used the bootroom for debriefing and planning sessions. "Every Sunday morning, we would come into Anfield and spend about an hour talking about the game. Even if we had won, we would usually discuss how to improve the team and make sure we didn't get complacent."

Roy Evans said: "It was just a room where we chatted about football. It became legendary as a think-tank because we kept on being successful and buying good players.

"It was great to sit there with a beer or a cup of tea, but in the end it was a mutual thought society."

Measuring 12ft x 12ft, it had no airs or graces, with merely a cupboard plus a few photos and calendars on the wall. When press photographers were allowed in, cupboard doors would be opened to hide any calendars that featured pin-up girls.

The players were not allowed in, but guests from opposing teams were.

PRESS ROOM

Changing times: The bootroom
was demolished in 1993 to make
way for the press room

Above: An Anfield stadium guide informs guests about the press room's hidden history

Below: Fernando Torres is unveiled to the press as a Liverpool player

One visitor was Elton John when he was Watford chairman in the 1980s. Elton reportedly asked for a pink gin when he was offered a drink but had to make do with a beer.

The bootroom was demolished in 1993 and then-manager Graeme Souness was wrongly accused of being responsible. In fact, it was a board decision, as they required bigger press facilities ahead of the European Championship matches staged at Anfield in 1996.

The area where the bootroom stood continues to be used by journalists for domestic games in 2010. It is here where the manager's post-match press conference is staged after Premier League, FA Cup and Carling Cup matches.

For European games, when the media contingent is substantially larger, the trophy room is used for press conferences. This is also where some significant signings have been unveiled and a couple of managers have said goodbye.

A slightly awe-struck Fernando Torres was presented to the media here, as were Xabi Alonso and Luis Garcia before him. Going further back, the collective summer signings of 1999 and 2000 were introduced in the trophy room, among them Sami Hyypia, Stephane Henchoz and Gary McAllister.

In November 1998 Roy Evans' 33-year association with Liverpool formally came to an end at a press conference in the trophy room. Following the dissolution of his managerial partnership with Gerard Houllier, Evans said he rejected the opportunity of another role within the club because he didn't want to become "a ghost on the wall".

Five-and-a-half years later Houllier himself was sat in the same room at the end of his period as manager. He reflected on his favourite memories, among them the 2001 FA Cup and UEFA Cup finals, watching the 'GH' mosaic being unveiled by the Kop soon after he fell ill, and his return for the Roma game in March 2002. Houllier closed the conference by vowing: "I will always remain a fan." Within a few weeks Rafael Benitez was being unveiled and a new era began.

INSIDE THE
DRESSING ROOM

GETTING READY FOR BATTLE BEHIND CLOSED DOORS »

WALK in the Anfield dressing room and you can almost feel the presence of the great names who have passed through over the years.

Bill Shankly, Ron Yeats, Kevin Keegan, Bob Paisley, Kenny Dalglish, Ian Rush, John Barnes, Robbie Fowler, Steven Gerrard, Jamie Carragher, Fernando Torres… to name but a few. The list is virtually endless.

The dressing rooms have a few modern additions but the structure and overall look remain the same as when Shankly was in charge.

This is where Liverpool's players have spent the final tense minutes before numerous big matches, listening to the inspirational words delivered by the manager. It is where everyone involved has celebrated wildly afterwards.

As you walk in, the players' shirts hang from hooks and you can see where each of them sits and gets changed.

One of the rules of the dressing room is that all players must speak English, even if it's a conversation between two Spanish speakers.

Motivational slogans stare at the players from the wall. One relating to teamwork reads as follows:

Coming together is a beginning
Keeping together is progress
Working together is success

All smiles: Bob Paisley jokes with Tommy Smith after a home game

There are reminders of other rules and regulations that have to be followed on the pitch. One poster tells players to 'Respect the ref', while another reminds them not to wear jewellery.

The players have easy access to a fridge containing isotonic drinks and water so they can ensure their energy levels are high during games and can be replenished afterwards.

There is a door in the dressing room that leads to Rafael Benitez's private room, which is used by the manager when he needs some time alone to gather his thoughts. It remains locked and mystery surrounds what is inside.

The home dressing room is actually smaller than the one used by away teams. Steven Gerrard prefers a slightly claustrophobic atmosphere. "It's good to be closer together, more tight-knit if you like, before we go out."

Inside the away dressing room, shirt designs of opponents from famous Anfield games hang on the wall. Printed on them are details of what happened during these matches.

The occasions commemorated include the 4-0 victory against Real Madrid in 2009, the 2005 Champions League semi-final win over Chelsea and the 1977 European Cup quarter-final when St Etienne were vanquished.

In all those matches, the din that reverberated from the stands overwhelmed the away team. The Anfield roar becomes even louder when leaving the dressing rooms and moving into the tunnel…

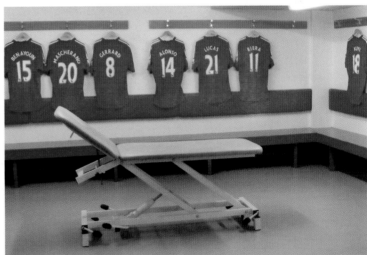

Left: Ronnie Moran, Kenny Dalglish and Roy Evans celebrate winning the league title in May 1990

Above: How the room looked in the 2008/09 season and, top, how it looked in the 1980s

Changing moods: Left, John Aldridge pours a drink over
Steve McMahon's head while Peter Beardsley looks on after
the league title was won in 1988
Above: Ian Rush listens to a team talk in the '80s

Bill Shankly rallies his troops in the
Anfield dressing room in the 1970s

Time to relax: John Aldridge takes a break from scoring goals in the Anfield dressing room in the 1980s

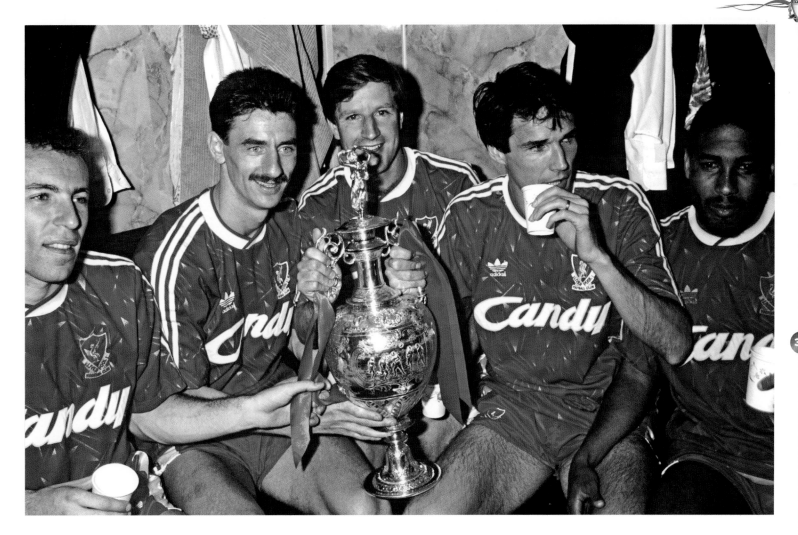

"There weren't any superstars in the dressing room. They were just great guys. The camaraderie, the good times, the laughs... that's one thing I miss about Liverpool. I miss going into the dressing room every day"

Alan Hansen

TUNNEL VISION

AS THE KOP REACHES FULL VOICE, THE PLAYERS TAKE THE FINAL WALK FROM THE DRESSING ROOMS TOWARDS THE HALLOWED ANFIELD TURF

This Is Anfield

**LINING UP BEHIND THE CAPTAINS,
READY TO FACE THE WALL OF NOISE »**

THOSE final seconds in the players' tunnel before walking out onto the pitch are when players are first exposed to what Anfield is all about.

Standing in the cramped corridor, waiting for the appropriate moment to go through and head towards the wall of noise.

For Liverpool players it is an inspiring experience, while the opposition can often be intimidated.

In 2005, Chelsea were shaken by the strength of the roar prior to the Champions League semi-final, as their captain John Terry admitted.

"When we heard the noise, I think we took it in too much and it affected us. I'm not saying we were frightened but it is an intimidating atmosphere."

Steven Gerrard says he likes to clear his thoughts and compose himself when he's standing in the tunnel.

"I like to get into the tunnel and just think about that game, nothing else. I like to know exactly what I've got to do and have my mind totally focused on the game.

"It's a sign of respect to shake hands with the other captain and maybe with the officials. But you won't see me turning round talking to anyone as it can take away from the focus."

Immediately in front of the players before they clatter down the steps is the 'This is Anfield' sign, originally put in place by Bill Shankly in the 1960s. Ever since, it has been superstition for Liverpool's players to lift their arms and touch the sign immediately before entering the field.

The sign is a statement, a stark reminder to opposition players exactly where they are and the standards to which they must aspire. Some of them touch the sign too, hoping they might be blessed with some of its magic qualities. Former Manchester United striker Andy Cole said he would look at it and think: "This is it, what it's all about."

The dugout

WHERE THE MANAGER SITS
TO SURVEY THE ACTION »

THE Anfield bench is where Liverpool's manager anxiously watches his players, sat just in front of the fans in the Main Stand.

In Rafael Benitez's case, he spends as much time on his feet as in his seat. The Spaniard is famous for how animated he gets when moving forward into the technical area, shouting, pointing and gesticulating.

He has always lived and breathed every moment on the pitch, making notes when, however briefly, he walks back to sit down.

Gerard Houllier was often on his feet during matches but it was his assistant, Phil Thompson, who would do most of the shouting, whistling to get players' attention from the edge of the touchline.

Most Liverpool managers have decided to watch games from close to the action; as well as Benitez and Houllier, it has been the chosen method for Roy Evans, Graeme Souness and Kenny Dalglish. As we mentioned earlier in this publication, Bill Shankly preferred to be in the directors' box, and so did Joe Fagan and Bob Paisley.

In the days when Anfield still had an old-fashioned dugout (it was replaced by uncovered seats in the mid-1990s), Dalglish was famous for being perched on the edge, half in and half out, anxiously surveying the scene in front of him.

Gunners downed: Arrowsmith scores against Arsenal in 1964

Liverpool 5 Arsenal 0
Football League Division One
April 18 1964

A first league championship for 17 years (and the first under Bill Shankly) was secured with a spectacular demolition of the Gunners.

The 48,000 fans who made it into Anfield were in for a treat. Ian St John, Alf Arrowsmith, Peter Thompson (2) and Roger Hunt put Liverpool five up by the hour mark. It could have been even more, as Ian Callaghan had a penalty saved after the fifth goal had been scored.

The championship trophy was not present so Liverpool's players made do with parading the 'Curlett Cup', a homemade trophy created by a family of Reds' supporters.

Liverpool 3 Inter Milan 1
European Cup semi-final, first leg
May 4 1965

The injured Gordon Milne and Gerry Byrne paraded the FA Cup, won for the first time just three days earlier at Wembley, before kick-off at a packed Anfield where an amazing atmosphere shook the Italian champions.

With noise levels reaching a frenzy never before heard inside an English stadium, Roger Hunt gave Liverpool the lead, but Mazzola equalised following a mistake by Ron Yeats.

However, with the Kop in full voice – they famously sang for Inter to "go back to Italy" to the tune of Santa Lucia – Bill Shankly's side scored twice more through Ian Callaghan (left) and Ian St John on Anfield's first great European night.

Only a highly controversial 3-0 defeat in the San Siro owing to several dubious refereeing decisions ended hopes of an appearance in the final.

Wash-out: The first leg at Anfield was initially abandoned after 27 minutes

Liverpool 3
Borussia Moenchengladbach 0
UEFA Cup final, first leg
May 10 1973

A huge downpour flooded the Anfield pitch and forced Austrian referee Erich Linemayr to abandon the game after 27 minutes, so it was replayed the following night with Bill Shankly making a key tactical change.

Shanks had spotted that Moenchengladbach were weak in the air and brought in big John Toshack for little Brian Hall – a plan that worked wonders as Toshack created two first-half goals for Kevin Keegan.

Larry Lloyd headed home a third to give the Reds a three-goal advantage – which was preserved by a crucial Ray Clemence penalty save – and although they were beaten 2-0 in Germany in the second leg, the club's first piece of European silverware was secured.

Liverpool 3 **Bruges 2**
UEFA Cup final, first leg
April 28 1976

It wasn't quite a comeback of Istanbul proportions, but it wasn't far off as the Belgians raced into a 2-0 lead after just 12 minutes.

Bob Paisley's decision to bring Jimmy Case on for John Toshack changed the game, and goals in the 59th and 61st minutes from Ray Kennedy and Case levelled matters.

With the Kop now in full voice, Liverpool continued to push, and in the 64th minute Steve Heighway was fouled in the box and Kevin Keegan converted the penalty to complete an amazing six-minute turnaround.

The Kop celebrated the goal wildly, and although Bruges took an early lead again in the second leg, Keegan fired home a free-kick to secure Liverpool's second UEFA Cup success in four seasons.

Liverpool 3 St Etienne 1
European Cup third round, second leg
March 16 1977

After losing 1-0 in France to a side widely regarded as the best in Europe at the time, Bob Paisley's men needed to win by two clear goals at Anfield.

Kevin Keegan opened the scoring after just two minutes but Dominique Bathenay equalised early in the second half.

Ray Kennedy made it 2-1, and with just six minutes remaining, supersub David Fairclough charged through to put the ball into the net in front of an ecstatic Kop.

It was a night that rocked Anfield to the rafters and ultimately paved the way to the glory of Rome and Liverpool's first European Cup triumph.

Liverpool 3 Everton 2
Football League Division One
November 21 1970

Bill Shankly had a team in transition, with youngsters Steve Heighway and John Toshack being introduced to the side – and what an impact they made here.

Goals from Alan Whittle and Joe Royle meant Everton led 2-0 deep into the second half before the Reds came roaring back.

A fantastic run by Heighway ended with him poking the ball past Andy Rankin to make it 2-1. He then provided an inviting cross for John Toshack, who headed his first goal for the club to level it up.

The Kop was already in full cry when Chris Lawler won it to crown a fabulous Liverpool fightback.

Heading for history: McDermott concludes a sweeping move by scoring our seventh against Spurs

Liverpool 7 Tottenham Hotspur 0
Football League Division One
September 2 1978

One of Liverpool's greatest teams produced their definitive performance in destroying a Tottenham team featuring World Cup winners Ossie Ardiles and Ricky Villa.

Kenny Dalglish had two within 20 minutes, re-directing Jimmy Case shots on both occasions. Ray Kennedy headed the third, helped by a deflection off Spurs' John Lacy.

Substitute David Johnson then scored two of his own, with Dalglish playing a significant role in both goals. When Steve Heighway was brought down in the area, Phil Neal saw his penalty saved, but a re-take was ordered by the referee and he made no mistake second time around, stretching the lead to 6-0.

The seventh goal was sublime. A fast, flowing move featuring Ray Kennedy, Dalglish and Johnson, it concluded with Terry McDermott heading home Heighway's perfect cross.

"One of Liverpool's greatest teams produced their definitive performance in destroying a Tottenham team featuring World Cup winners"

44

Liverpool 4 **Newcastle United 3**
FA Premier League
April 3 1996

At an awards ceremony to celebrate the first 10 years of the Premier League, this match was voted Game of the Decade.

If you were at Anfield that night, you'll understand why. The game was played at a frenetic pace, spurred on by Robbie Fowler's opening goal in the second minute. Kevin Keegan's Newcastle, who were fighting for the title, came back strongly, twice taking the lead and twice being pegged back.

With the score locked at 3-3, Stan Collymore slammed in the winner in the final minute to send the Kop into a frenzy.

Liverpool 3 **Olympiakos 1**
Champions League group stage one
December 9 2004

With Liverpool needing to win 1-0 or by two clear goals to progress to the knockout stage of the Champions League in Rafa Benitez's first season at the club, Rivaldo stunned Anfield with a first-half free-kick to leave the Reds needing a miracle.

But a couple of inspired substitutions by Benitez turned the game on its head, with Florent Sinama-Pongolle equalising in the 47th minute and Neil Mellor making it 2-1 with just nine minutes left.

Liverpool still needed a goal and it was inspirational captain Steven Gerrard who provided it when he smashed a stunning half-volley into the Kop net from 20 yards out to begin some of the wildest celebrations Anfield had seen in years.

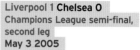

Liverpool 1 Chelsea 0
Champions League semi-final,
second leg
May 3 2005

On an atmospheric night to rival anything ever produced in the 1960s and 1970s, Rafa Benitez's Liverpool booked their place in the Champions League final with a single-goal victory over recently crowned Premiership champions Chelsea.

After a 0-0 draw at Stamford Bridge the visitors were favourites, but a controversial fourth-minute goal from Luis Garcia – which Chelsea claimed never crossed the line but was awarded by Slovakian linesman Roman Slysko – was enough to settle the tie.

Chelsea pushed for an equaliser but a stubborn rearguard display, led by the outstanding Jamie Carragher, kept them at bay, and when the full-time whistle went Anfield erupted to celebrate Liverpool reaching their first European Cup final for 20 years.

Three weeks later and more than 40,000 travelling Kopites were celebrating a fifth European Cup triumph after a penalty shoot-out victory over AC Milan, following a comeback of epic proportions.

45

THE LIVERPOOL FC EXPERIENCE

THE KOP

**THE MOST FAMOUS
STAND IN THE WORLD**

ALAN KENNEDY, FORMER LIVERPOOL PLAYER

You never knew how many were in the old Kop. Allegedly, there were 25,000 but I think there could be more for really big games.

They affectionately nicknamed me 'Barney Rubble', maybe because I played like The Flintstones character; running through walls and giving everything.

The Kop was so vociferous. They used to chant our names and get behind us. At times that ball used to be sucked into the back of the net. Maybe they came to expect us to win every game at Anfield but sometimes that wasn't the case. One of the good things about it was they always gave the opposing goalkeeper a round of applause. In 1981/82, when we won the league against Tottenham, Ray Clemence came back and they gave him a great round of applause. I think that gees goalkeepers up.

When players saw all those people on the Kop, the hair stood up on the back of the neck. I'm sure some just froze at Anfield but it often also brought out the best in people.

Let me tell you a story

OF A CHURCH, COMMUNITY CENTRE AND WAY OF LIFE, ALL ROLLED INTO ONE »

SPION Kop.

It's arguably the most famous suburb in Liverpool.

Never mind Edge Hill, Kensington, West Derby, Toxteth, Huyton, Walton, Aigburth, Anfield or anywhere else.

If you asked a Liverpudlian where he came from in the '60s, '70s or '80s, then he'd tell you: 'Spion Kop.'

Mind you, when you've got a messiah leading the club like Bill Shankly – who once filled in a form and put his address down as 'Anfield' – then it's no wonder that followers of Liverpool Football Club had an affinity with the Kop.

And that's what the famous stand is all about – Kopites. The group of people who turned what was once just a pile of cinder into the most famous, most feared, most respected and most celebrated terracing in world football.

Manchester United had the Stretford End. Arsenal the North Bank. You'd find Evertonians on the Gwladys Street and Geordies in the Gallowgate End.

Famous? In their own right. But not a patch on the Spion Kop.

Even now, in the era of all-seater stadia, The Kop remains the most famous stand in any English football ground.

Liverpool and the Kop go hand in hand.

To the tabloid headline writers, the Kop IS Liverpool. How many other clubs do you see regularly referred to in the press by the name on one of their stands? None.

That's the impact, the lasting effect on the minds of those not associated with Liverpool, that the Kop has had. Anyone who stood on it will tell you that's not surprising.

The Kop was more than concrete and steel. More than an imposing structure that dominated the Anfield skyline. It was a church. A community centre. A way of life. All rolled into one.

Kopites didn't just attend Anfield for the football, they came for everything else that went with it too. They came, in droves, to stand on the Spion Kop. Their Kop. The laughs, the banter, the spirit. The status of being a Kopite.

Singing, shouting, chanting, celebrating, cat-calling and banter. Those 25,000 Reds stood shoulder to shoulder, breathing down the visiting goalkeeper's neck.

Visiting goalies didn't just have what Liverpool put in front of them to contend with. They had an entire stand trying to suck the ball into the net behind them. They were intimidating without being nasty. They didn't need to be.

The noise and size of the support was enough in itself to have grown men trembling in their boots. Standing on the Kop wasn't a place for the faint-hearted to be either.

One current banner seen around the fields of Anfield Road in recent times says simply: 'Above Us, Only Sky.' The quote, from a John Lennon classic, didn't apply to the Kop. As well as the impressive and imposing steel roof, plumes of cigarette smoke would drift upwards into the air.

On some nights you could see steam rising off the Kop, like there was a cauldron on the boil behind the goal. Things would reach boiling point when Liverpool scored.

A crescendo of noise erupted as the Kop surged forward. It was bedlam. You'd find yourself carried forward and not be able to do anything about it.

Then, when the surge relented, you'd be carried back to somewhere near

TOMMY SMITH, FORMER LIVERPOOL CAPTAIN

IN the '60s, Liverpool was the centre of the universe. The Beatles were just starting out and Merseyside was booming at that time. The Kop invented all these songs and chants that had no equal in football.

For me, it's where it all began. The whole world copied the Kop, but there was only one genuine article.

You'd go to take a throw-in and there were always hundreds of people shouting advice and telling you what do.

It was like having 25,000 coaches at one end of the ground, all very knowledgeable in their own right.

Liverpudlians know their football, no doubt about that.

When you look at footage of the standing Kop at its peak, it's an awesome sight. Of course, Bill Shankly was the undisputed King of the Kop. He loved them and they loved him. Shanks always wanted to be one of them. He actually went in the Kop at the end of his career on one occasion. The thing I remember was one of those famous days when we paraded another trophy around the pitch.

Kopites were throwing their red scarves onto the track for us to pick up. Shanks already had a couple around his neck. A policeman kicked one aside and the boss was furious. He let the copper know in no uncertain terms.

Shanks demanded that the fans were treated with the utmost respect. The Kop was pure gold as far as he was concerned and it was the same for me. I've been lucky enough to travel all over the world. You can be thousands of miles away and walking down the street and someone will suddenly recognise you.

The first thing they ask is: "What was it like to play for Liverpool FC?" The second thing they ask is: "What was it like to play in front of the Kop?"

It's an easy answer for me. "Absolutely wonderful."

The Kop was as much a part of Liverpool's success as the team.

Just like my old boss Shanks, I hold them in the highest regard.

Red and white panorama: The view from the back of the Kop

to where you started. Finding your favourite spec on the Kop was one thing, staying in it for the full 90 minutes was another.

If Liverpool was the Capital of Culture in 2008 then the Kop was football's cultural capital for decades. It led the way in terms of noise, singing, colour, humour, chanting, ingenuity and even fashion. The rest have been playing catch-up ever since.

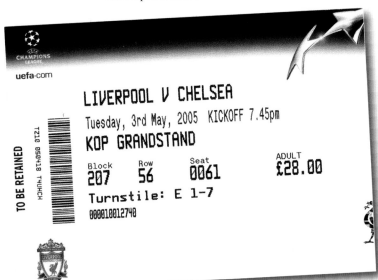

Left: A Kop ticket from the incredible Champions League semi-final against Chelsea in 2005

KENNY DALGLISH

There was a unique bond between the people who stood on the terraces of the Kop and the players that they came to watch. It was a relationship that I believe was built on mutual respect.

The fans respected the players because they were successful. We won things almost every season and as a fan all you want for your team is for them to make you proud and to win silverware. The players gave their everything, every week, and their efforts did not go unappreciated.

There was no better lift when you were a goal down and chasing the game than the Kop in full voice. They got us through some tricky times and that unswerving support was part of what endeared the support to the players. But we, as players, also knew that we were living the dreams of the people watching from the stands. They would have traded everything to be where we were so we wanted success for them as well as ourselves.

You would go that extra mile for them because they would go that extra mile for you in return. Playing in front of the Kop was an experience few people will ever forget.

51

BRIAN HALL, FORMER LIVERPOOL PLAYER

I remember the first time I came across the Kop. It was in 1962, the year they went up to the First Division, and they had an epic FA Cup tie with Preston North End.

They drew at Anfield, drew at Preston and went to Manchester for a third game which Preston won by a Peter Thompson goal.

But we were invaded at Preston by Liverpool fans on the night of the second game. It's one of the most memorable football nights I ever had. It was incredible. The banter, the noise, the songs, the chants, the humour – it was just absolutely fabulous.

By 1965 I'd signed on as an amateur, and after training Reuben Bennett came to us and said: "I've got some passes if you want to watch the game tonight." It was a European game, I can't remember who against, and I got there for half-time.

We went on the paddock and I spent most of the 45 minutes watching the Kop. I'd never seen anything like it in my life. It was absolutely phenomenal. The songs, the noise and the steam coming off it – it was just out of this world.

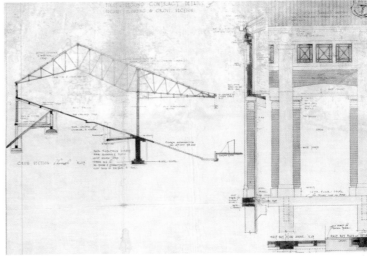

HOW THE SPION KOP GOT ITS NAME »

DEFEAT isn't a word that was particularly associated with the Spion Kop. However, it was defeat for a group of Liverpudlian soldiers that played a significant part in giving the famous old terrace its name.

In January 1900, scores of Scousers were part of the Lancashire Fusiliers that went to battle in the Boer War.

A fierce battle took place on a hill near Ladysmith, South Africa, that was known locally as Spioenkop Hill. The battle ended in defeat with more than 322 men losing their lives, many of whom were from the Lancashire Fusiliers.

Six years later and that South African hill would become part of Merseyside folklore forever. The Kop itself was built as a reward for Liverpool supporters after the club lifted its second league championship in 1906. Anfield already had a small terraced area at the Walton Breck Road end but chairman John Houlding and club secretary 'Honest' John McKenna decided there was room for improvement.

A steep, cinder bank with wooden steps and no roof was designed by well-respected architect Archibald Leitch and constructed that summer. All they needed now was a name. At first they were, like a batsman out of his crease, well and truly stumped.

'Walton Breck Bank' sounded like something where you kept your shillings, while they'd have never fitted 'The Walton Breck Road end' on match tickets.

The season kicked off and the new stand, which held around 20,000 spectators and gave some splendid views across Stanley Park, remained nameless.

It has been suggested (though there is no concrete proof) that it was Ernest Edwards, sports editor of the Liverpool Echo at the time, who had a moment of inspiration during that campaign.

Edwards allegedly said that Liverpool's new terracing reminded him of the hill where the battle of Ladysmith had taken place, so why not call the stand the Spion Kop?

There could have been a very different response if the battle had taken place on Mount Kilimanjaro but, as it was, the name stuck.

However, Liverpool's wasn't the first Kop.

The same title had previously been given to terracing at Woolwich Arsenal but the name never caught on.

Arsenal's old North Bank gives you an idea of what could have been for Anfield if it wasn't for Edwards.

His suggestion was probably greeted with such enthusiasm because local men had lost their lives on Spioenkop Hill.

It was almost as if a belated memorial had been put up in Liverpool and everyone liked it.

A 1-0 win over Stoke on September 1, in blazing-hot heat, was watched by 30,000 fans with many becoming the first to ever watch a game from the Kop.

Anfield may have initially been Everton's ground but their supporters never stood on the Kop as we know it.

For the eight years they played at Anfield – between 1884 and 1892 – their supporters had to make do with that unremarkable terracing on Walton Breck Road.

BILL SHANKLY, FORMER LIVERPOOL MANAGER

Liverpool was made for me and I was made for Liverpool, and I knew that the people who mattered most were the ones who came through the turnstiles.

A manager has got to identify himself with the people. Football is their whole life, and for the last 12 seasons Liverpool have played two games most weeks, which is hard on the pocket.

The encouragement the supporters of Liverpool Football Club have given their team has been incredible.

When there is a corner-kick at the Kop end of the ground they frighten the ball! Occasionally I would have a walk round the ground before a match, and I went to the Kop one day before it had filled up.

A little chap there said: "Stand here, Bill, you'll get a good view of the game from here!" I couldn't take him up on that offer because I had to look after the team.

I have watched a match from the Kop since I retired as team manager, and that was just the start of going to see the supporters in all parts of the ground. I didn't go to the Kop for bravado or anything like that. I went as a mark of respect for the people who had been good to me.

They used to chant my name as much as they chanted the names of the players, which was unusual. I am a working man and I went among my own kind.

Liverpool played Coventry that day, and a crescendo greeted the Liverpool team just as I went into the ground.

It wasn't a great game and we only drew that day, so there wasn't a continuous din.

But when we scored our goal the noise was deafening.

Open to the elements:
The unroofed Spion Kop

The Kop was entirely a Liverpool institution and the next major change came in 1928, largely thanks to the British weather.

Standing on the Kop with 20,000 other people was one thing. Standing on it in torrential rain, gale force winds or even through thunder and lightning was another.

The roofless Kop was an unpleasant place to be on a dreadful day, even for hardened dockers who'd regularly be battered by the elements down by the Mersey.

The prospect of soggy flat caps and wet ciggies all round wasn't exactly going to attract people to Anfield, so the board of directors decided the time had come to build a roof.

Mr J Watson Cabre, an architect from Great Crosby, was put in charge of the new development and by the start of the 1928/29 season Anfield had the first roofed-in Kop in the country.

Part of the terracing was also redeveloped during the construction work so apart from the cinder hill beneath the terracing and three concrete staircases, Kopites had virtually a brand new home.

Up to 28,000 fans could now be accommodated, and the roof – 80 feet high, 425 feet long and 131 feet wide – dominated the Anfield skyline.

The outside walls and six internal stanchions of the Kop were said to carry a massive 45,500 square feet of roof space – into which 91 standard houses could be packed together in one layer.

It was a big roof for a big club who had big ambitions.

As the roof went up, so did the entrance price. It now cost one shilling (five pence) to stand on the Kop.

You couldn't afford one of Fernando Torres' eyelashes for five pence these days but, nonetheless, that was still a hefty price for the majority to pay, particularly as unemployment was beginning to bite on Merseyside.

The new-look Kop was officially opened by the President of the Football League, and former secretary, director and chairman of the club, John McKenna on August 25.

Liverpool beat Bury 3-0 that day in front of 40,000 fans and McKenna was reportedly presented with a gold cigar to mark the occasion.

Far more significant for the 40,000 who weren't presented with gold cigars was the moment when Billy Millar opened the scoring for Liverpool.

With just 50 seconds on the clock Millar headed home and the new Kop erupted for the first time.

It was like a volcano had gone off. The acoustics were fantastic, the noise was something else.

The Kop had a wall like no other in football – a wall of noise.

Not only had putting a roof over the terracing stopped the rain from getting in, it had stopped the noise from getting out.

Liverpool Football Club had a 12th man.

But it would be another 30 years or so, and the inspiration of one man, Bill Shankly, before they got the best out of him.

The 12th man: The roof kept the weather out and the noise in

SIR BOBBY ROBSON, FORMER MANAGER

I loved Liverpool. I just thought it was a great cathedral and a great place to play. I remember the old Kop, which went back bloody miles. I don't know how many it held – maybe 18-20,000 – everybody standing.

Those are the days that I remember; the swell of the Kop, the surge of the Kop, the singing of the Kop. Oh, it was a great place. I enjoyed going to Liverpool when I was with Ipswich. I never won. I remember getting a 3-3 draw one day. They were great days.

It always seems to be a cauldron there. The roar of the Kop; the enthusiasm within the public. It spills onto the pitch, I think.

There was always a smell of adrenalin at Liverpool, I tell you. I just think it's been one of the great stadiums of all time, for years and years and years. You have produced, over the years, fantastic teams.

ANFIELD TREASURES

THE LIVERPOOL FC MUSEUM ENABLES YOU TO WALK THROUGH THE
CLUB'S UNPARALLELED HISTORY. HERE WE HIGHLIGHT A SELECTION
OF SOME OF THE MOST SIGNIFICANT ITEMS IN OUR COLLECTION

'The Old Lady'

FIRST DIVISION CHAMPIONSHIP

WINNERS

1900-01	1905-06	1921-22	1922-23	1946-47	1963-64
1965-66	1972-73	1975-76	1976-77	1978-79	1979-80
1981-82	1982-83	1983-84	1985-86	1987-88	1989-90

The Liverpool FC birth certificate

Where it all began. Dated June 3 1892, this certificate, issued by the Board of Trade, officially marks the birth of what was to become the most successful club in English football history. Everything you read about in this book follows from this single sheet of paper.

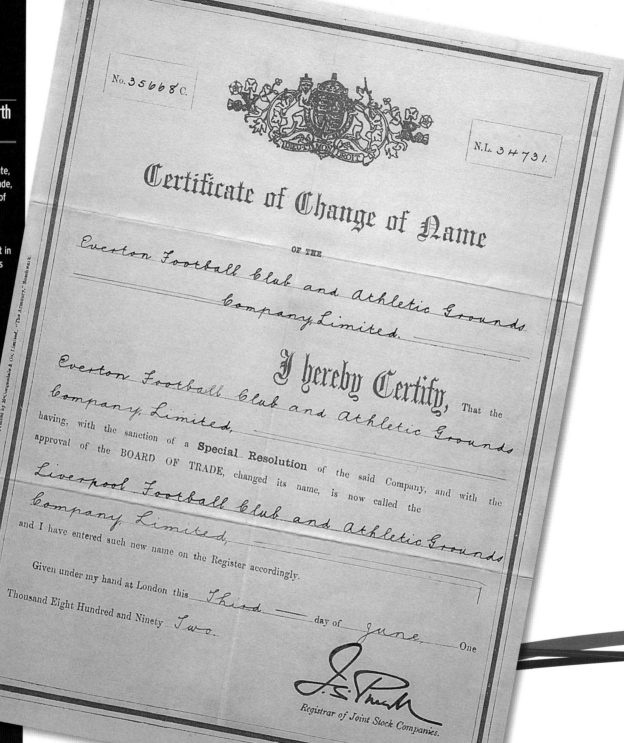

No. 35668 C.

N.L. 34731.

Certificate of Change of Name

OF THE

Everton Football Club and Athletic Grounds Company, Limited.

I hereby Certify, That the Everton Football Club and Athletic Grounds Company, Limited, having, with the sanction of a **Special Resolution** of the said Company, and with the approval of the BOARD OF TRADE, changed its name, is now called the Liverpool Football Club and Athletic Grounds Company, Limited, and I have entered such new name on the Register accordingly.

Given under my hand at London this _Third_ day of _June_, One Thousand Eight Hundred and Ninety _Two._

Registrar of Joint Stock Companies.

2005

A salvaged slab from the original Spion Kop

Salvaged when the terrace was demolished in 1994, this was once a small part of the most famous stand in football. The club also has in its possession a white stone removed from the summit of the actual Spioenkop in South Africa, where native and British forces fought a two-day battle in 1900 during the Boer war. A newly constructed mound at Anfield was given the name 'Spion Kop' – to discover how it got this name, turn to page 53.

Champions League final match ball

One of a number used during that unforgettable evening in Istanbul, this ball was picked up by a steward as soon as the penalty shoot-out was over, and, subsequently, was purchased by the club from a private collector. The scuff marks testify to its use but we don't know at which stage of the game it was in play. Perhaps the six-minute spell leading up to the hour mark?

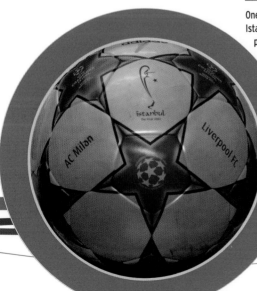

A ball from the greatest European Cup final of them all

Bob Paisley's cap

Liverpool's most successful manager wore a number of flat caps during his time in charge at Anfield and this is one of them, worn frequently pitch-side and in training. So attached to caps was Paisley that he insisted on taking a new one to Rome for the 1977 European Cup final. Wife Jessie warned him it would be an unnecessary accompaniment because of the balmy Italian temperatures, but Bob stubbornly insisted on travelling with the cap, and, as predicted by Jessie, it proved too warm to be worn!

1965

Match programme for European Cup semi-final away leg v Inter Milan

This match is notorious amongst Liverpool fans because Inter Milan went through to the final in dubious circumstances. The first leg, played three days after the Reds had won the FA Cup for the first time, took place in an incredible Anfield atmosphere, but the 3-1 victory on the night proved not to be enough. Amid (unsubstantiated) accusations of bribery, Inter won 3-0 at the San Siro: one goal going straight in from an indirect free-kick and another coming when goalkeeper Tommy Lawrence was robbed of the ball whilst bouncing it. It was a lesson in gamesmanship.

1977

Ticket for European Cup quarter-final v St Etienne

This would have gained you entrance to the Kemlyn Road (now Centenary) stand for one of the greatest Anfield nights. In fact, it is generally accepted that the St Etienne game is one of the definitive top three matches played at our ground. It was the night David Fairclough wrote himself into club history as commentator Gerald Sinstadt roared: "Supersub strikes again!"

Liverpool Football Club

LIVERPOOL F.C.

v.

ST. ETIENNE F.C.
(FRANCE)

16th MARCH, 1977

Kemlyn Road Stand
Block "J"

Row	Seat No.
№ 26	121

This portion to be retained.

Issued Subject to the Rules and Regs. of the Football Association

LIVERPOOL FOOTBALL CLUB

European Champion Clubs' Cup Competition
Quarter Final   ::   Second Leg

LIVERPOOL F C v. **ST. ETIENNE F C**
(FRANCE)

AT ANFIELD
WEDNESDAY, 16th MARCH, 1977
Kick-off 7-30 p.m.

KEMLYN ROAD STAND
Block J

ADMISSION £3.00 (including VAT)	Row	Seat No.
	№ 26	121

P. B. Robinson
Secretary.

This Portion to be given up at turnstiles.

Carra's winning medal

This is part of the incredible collection of all Jamie Carragher's medals to date, which are on display in the museum. Jamie chose to hand them over for display without being asked.

Celebration Dinner
Menu card from the 'Double' celebration dinner held in the Adelphi Hotel on 20th July 1973. A glorious peak in the career of Bill Shankly.

Rafa's Bag
Rafa Benitez famously keeps notes about all aspects of the game and his players.
This bag carried them to every stage, including to the final.

2004/05

Rafael Benitez's Champions League leather bag

The Spaniard carried this holdall with him throughout his first season in charge at Liverpool, including to all the European ties, and kept his famous notes inside it. The bag was donated to the museum a few months after the Champions League final when Benitez decided to buy a new one.

1896/97

Liverpool season ticket stub

This is the oldest LFC ticket in the club's possession (actually it is the receipt). It is on loan from a private collector, Douglas Wix of Liverpool. In that season the Reds finished fifth in a 16-team First Division.

A Liddell bit of history

Many from the older generation of Reds' supporters consider Liddell to be greatest player to have graced Anfield. This is his first professional contract, signed on April 17 1939 when Liddell was just 17. The outbreak of war five months later delayed his first-team debut until 1946, by which time Liddell was 24. Despite the late start, he went on to make 534 appearances and scored 228 goals. His final match came in 1960 when he was 38. Fast and powerful, he could shoot with either foot and was a superb header of the ball. In short, Liddell was the complete player. He carried the club through the 1950s when they became known as 'Liddellpool'. He deserved to finish his career with far more than a single championship medal from 1946/47 and an FA Cup runners-up medal from 1950.

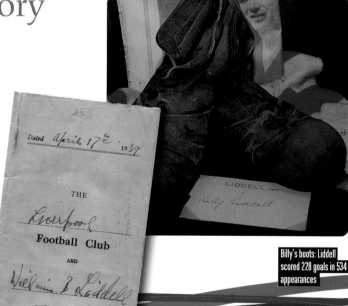

Billy's boots: Liddell scored 228 goals in 534 appearances

What a deal: Billy Liddell's first Liverpool contract from 1939

1892/93

Reserve league championship medal

Excluding the birth certificate, this is the oldest piece of Liverpool memorabilia in the museum. It is a reserve league winners' medal from 1892/93 – the club's first season. It was won by John P McNally, who made a number of appearances for the Reds' second string during that campaign. The silver medal is engraved with McNally's name and refers to the 'Liverpool League and District'. That season Liverpool's first team won the Lancashire League and were subsequently elected to the Football League, going on to win the Second Division at the first attempt.

Ticket for the last stand of the Kop, v Norwich, 1994

This is actually an unissued ticket for the final match in front of the famous terrace. Norwich pooped the party a little by winning 1-0, with Jeremy Goss scoring the final goal at the Kop end.

LIVERPOOL FOOTBALL CLUB

LIVERPOOL v. NORWICH CITY

SATURDAY, 30th APRIL, 1994

HOME SUPPORTERS ONLY

SPION KOP

ADULT

24 Hour Ticket & Match
Information 051-260 9999

THIS PORTION TO BE GIVEN UP AT TURNSTILES

№ 16480

F.A. CARLING PREMIERSHIP

YOU'LL NEVER WALK ALONE

LIVERPOOL FOOTBALL CLUB

EST. 1892

Carlsberg
LIVERPOOL

This Ticket is valid for this match on whatever date it may be played.

LIVERPOOL FOOTBALL CLUB

LIVERPOOL v. NORWICH CITY

AT ANFIELD

SATURDAY, 30th APRIL, 1994

KICK-OFF 3.00 pm

HOME SUPPORTERS ONLY

SPION KOP END

ADULT

ADMISSION £8.00 inc. VAT

THIS PORTION TO BE RETAINED

P. B. Robinson
Chief Executive/General Secretary

№ 16480

1984

1984 European Cup final ticket

What a stunning ticket this is, featuring an image of the King of Spades on the front. It would have got you into the Curva Nord at Rome's Olympic Stadium when Roma provided the opposition for what became Liverpool's fourth European Cup triumph. Susan Taberner, who worked for the museum for a number of years, donated it to the museum.

FINALE coppa dei campioni

ROMA/STADIO OLIMPICO 30 MAGGIO 1984/ORE 20.15

CURVA NORD
CANCELLO L

0002372

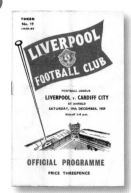

1959

Match programme for Bill Shankly's first game as manager

On December 19 1959 Liverpool hosted Cardiff City at Anfield in a Second Division fixture. The Reds were hammered 4-0 but the game was to develop an historical significance as it was the first one with Bill Shankly as manager.

Thank You Boss

An informal dinner party sponsored by Liverpool F.C. players to mark Mr. Bill Shankly's 15 years as manager.

St George's Hotel, Liverpool   August 21, 1974

'Thank You Boss': Tribute night to Bill Shankly, 1974

When Bill Shankly retired as Liverpool manager, the players organised a special tribute evening to him in August 1974. Staged at St George's Hotel in Liverpool, the menu included 'Cured Kop Cod' and an apology for the absence of haggis because "it is the close season". A note at the bottom adds: "Despite this, Boss, we hope you and Mrs Shanks have enjoyed the evening organised by players and staff as a small token of our appreciation."

The 'Old Lady' Football League championship trophy

There are few, if any, more majestic trophies than this. Liverpool won it 18 times, with their first title won in 1900/01 and the latest in 1989/90. Since the formation of the Premier League in 1992, the trophy is now awarded to the winners of the Championship (the old Second Division). The trophy you see here is a two-thirds scale silver replica that Liverpool were given special permission to create.

'The Old Lady'

FIRST DIVISION CHAMPIONSHIP

WINNERS

1900 - 01	1905-06	1921-22	1922-23	1946-47	1963-64
1965-66	1972-73	1975-76	1976-77	1978-79	1979-80
1981-82	1982-83	1983-84	1985-86	1987-88	1989-90

1966

Roger Hunt's World Cup medal

The only Liverpool player to have appeared in a World Cup final for the winning side is Roger Hunt, who featured in all six of England's matches in 1966, scoring three goals along the way. His winners' medal has been on display at the museum since 2003. However, he is no longer the only Liverpool player to own one: in 2009 fellow squad members Ian Callaghan and Gerry Byrne were presented with their own, 43 years late. In 1966 only the 11 who took part in the final were awarded a medal.

PAUL KRAMER
médailleur
NEUCHATEL

Parade: Hunt shows off the Jules Rimet World Cup trophy at Anfield

1900/01 league championship medal

This was won by Tom Robertson, a Scottish winger who was an ever-present during Liverpool's first championship-winning season, scoring nine goals. Back then the club actually commissioned the medals, as the Football League did not award a standard design, as such. Each winning club could add whatever embellishments they desired.

LEAGUE CHAMPIONSHIP
T. ROBERTSON FORWARD
SEASON 1900 1901

Albert Stubbins's 1946/47 league championship medal

Liverpool were crowned champions in the first season of a full Football League programme following the end of World War II. This is the medal awarded to striker Albert Stubbins, who scored 24 goals in 36 matches in 1946/47. A Geordie by birth, he arguably became the first hero of the Kop in the post-war era before Billy Liddell came fully to prominence. Long after his retirement, Stubbins was to feature among the montage of faces on the front cover of the Beatles' Sgt Pepper's Lonely Hearts Club Band album.

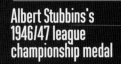

Rush scored one...

Ian Rush's 1992 FA Cup final shirt

Liverpool's greatest goalscorer (346) netted more memorable goals than the one he put past Sunderland keeper Tony Norman in the 1992 FA Cup final, but it would be remiss not to include him in this list. Rush won three FA Cups and had scored twice against Everton in the finals of 1986 and 1989. He added another against Sunderland in 1992 to round off a 2-0 victory.

Gerard Houllier's red scarf

When Houllier left Anfield in 2004 he was happy to hand over his iconic red scarf, which he wore so often whilst standing on the Anfield touchline. Apparently when the club took possession of the Nina Ricci lambswool product, it had a distinct whiff of cologne aftershave.

Bill Shankly's tracksuit top

This was given to the great man ahead of the 1974 FA Cup final, which proved to be Shankly's final match in charge of Liverpool before he announced his retirement. The old black jumper you can see underneath was a favourite of his and he often wore it during training at Melwood. It is a remarkable survivor, thanks to one of his granddaughters, who kept it safe.

L.F.C.
F.A. CUP FINAL
1974

Ian St John's 1965 FA Cup final shirt

Another fabulous garment. This Umbro top was worn by Ian St John in the 1965 FA Cup final against Leeds United. St John scored the winner in extra-time with a header from an Ian Callaghan cross. It hangs in a display case at the museum along with the match programme and a ticket to the game.

RE STADIUM · WEMB
● The Football Association
CUP COMPETITION
Final Tie
Saturday, May 1, 1965, kick off 3 p.m.
YOU ARE ADVISED TO TAKE UP YOUR POSITION BY 2.30 P.M.
CHAIRMAN: WEMBLEY STADIUM LTD

NORTH TERRACE   45/-

ENTER	ENTRANCE	ROW	SEAT
D	1	11	212
TURNSTILE	RIGHT		

RETAINED   (See Plan & Conditions on bac

Ticket to ride:
A pass into the 1965 FA
Cup final against Leeds

Joey Jones "frogs' legs" banner

The most famous banner in Liverpool's history is also one of the biggest. It is so big that it cannot be displayed in the club's museum at the moment, but hopefully that will change in the future. The banner was unfurled prior to the 1977 European Cup final in Rome when the Reds faced Borussia Moenchengladbach and paid tribute to Jones's unstinting commitment during the run to the final. It read: 'Joey ate the frogs' legs, made the Swiss roll, now he's munching Gladbach.' The men who created it gave it to Joey, who in turn loaned it to the club. Joey considers it to be the most precious reminder of his playing career.

Hansen with the Milk Cup in 1984 - his shirt in Rome was almost identical

Alan Hansen's 1984 European Cup final shirt

The shirt worn by 'Jocky' in Rome. It is one of many items on display at the museum that have been loaned by one of the club's greatest defenders, including his fabulous haul of medals.

Kevin Keegan's Stylo boots

These were worn by Keegan during his final season with Liverpool, 1976/77, when the Reds came so close to completing the treble, only missing out by losing the FA Cup final. Stylo boots were said to be extremely uncomfortable, and by the following year (when he was a Hamburg player) Keegan was wearing a pair of Patrick boots. Those boots are also on display in the museum, alongside his Hamburg Super Cup match shirt worn against Liverpool.

Close-up of Keegan's famous signature

The European Cup

There are five of them and this is the actual one raised to the sky in Istanbul in 2005. The most popular museum item of all, and it is Liverpool's to keep, forever! Following changes to UEFA rules, this is the last such trophy that will be presented to any football club, irrespective of how many finals they might win.

Alan Kennedy's 1984 European Cup final kit

The man whose left foot twice won the European Cup for Liverpool: in 1981 with the only goal against Real Madrid in Paris, and three years later at the conclusion of the penalty shoot-out in Rome. Kennedy's full kit from the 1984 final is on display at the museum.

AROUND THE
GROUND

**THE HISTORY OF ANFIELD EXTENDS BEYOND THE
STADIUM ITSELF AND INTO THE STREETS NEARBY**

Above: The Anfield pitch covered in flowers and
other tributes to the 96 supporters who lost their
lives in the Hillsborough disaster in 1989

Right: The Hillsborough memorial outside Anfield
and, far right, the Paisley Gateway

ALTHOUGH not part of the official tour of Anfield, there are a number of landmarks around the ground which have to be visited.

The *Hillsborough memorial*, immediately to the left of the *Shankly Gates* on Anfield Road, is the most poignant. Featuring an eternal flame at its centre, the memorial contains the full names and ages of the 96 Liverpool supporters who lost their lives at the FA Cup semi-final on April 15 1989.

Immediately after the disaster, thousands of people visited the ground and a carpet of flowers formed on the pitch and the Kop.

There are always flowers and wreaths placed at the foot of the memorial, and it's a place where fans of Liverpool and away teams come to reflect on matchdays.

The aforementioned Shankly Gates were erected in August 1982 in tribute to the legendary former manager Bill, who died less than a year earlier. His widow, Nessie, officially opened them. Above the gates stands the title of the club anthem: 'You'll Never Walk Alone'.

Outside the entrance to the museum and tour centre is an eight-foot *bronze statue of Shankly*, created by sculptor Tom Murphy, that depicts him with a fan's scarf around his neck and arms outstretched – his trademark pose. Inscribed on the statue's plinth are the words: 'Bill Shankly – He made the people happy.'

One of the entrances at the Kop end is the *Paisley Gateway*, which pays tribute to the Reds' most successful manager.

Three European Cups go across the top archway, while the gates have the crests of Paisley's birthplace, Hetton-le-Hole, and the Liverbird built into them. On the brick pillars at either side are an image of the man himself and a list of the honours he won while in charge of the Reds.

The Sandon Arms
and Stanley House

Back on Anfield Road, at number 73, is **Stanley House**, a striking red-brick building that was home to Liverpool's founder, John Houlding. It was while living here that he and his supporters planned the formation of a new club after the split with Everton.

Houlding, a brewer who owned his own pubs, had been Everton's landlord when they played at Anfield but conflict arose with the club's directors over a number of issues. One of them was Houlding's insistence that his own sparkling ales be sold at the ground.

The tipping point came when Houlding tried to increase the rent, and the Everton members responded by offering to pay a reduced amount.

The official split between Houlding and Everton took place on March 12 1892. He attempted to retain the Everton name but the Football Association and Football League refused to allow it.

On March 15, in Stanley House, Houlding discussed what to do next with people loyal to him, John McKenna and William Barclay. It was Barclay who suggested adopting the name 'Liverpool' to attract loyalty from across the city.

The Sandon public house stands on the corner of Oakfield Road and Walton Breck Road. It was owned by John Houlding and was used by Everton's players as changing facilities when Anfield was their home. When Liverpool took over the ground in 1892, they rented a house in Kemlyn Road in which the home and away teams could get changed, and this practice continued until 1894 when a new stand was erected. The Sandon remains one of the main gathering points for Liverpool supporters before and after matches.

BILL SHANKLY

He made the people happy

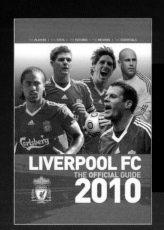

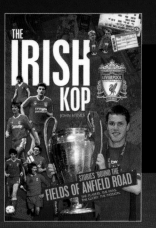
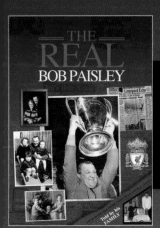
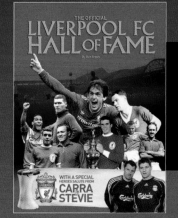